R-3363-DOE

A Reassessment of Potential Adversaries to U.S. Nuclear Programs

Bruce Hoffman, Peter deLeon
With Bonnie Cordes, Sue Ellen Moran, Thomas C. Tompkins

March 1986

Prepared for the
U.S. Department of Energy

1700 MAIN STREET
P.O. BOX 2138
SANTA MONICA, CA 90406-2138

U
264
.H64
1986

PREFACE

This report presents the results of a study undertaken as part of a larger research effort sponsored by the Inspector General of the U.S. Department of Energy (DOE) and administered by the Aerospace Corporation. The purpose of the study was to examine and assess the threat posed to U.S. nuclear weapons programs by politically and economically motivated adversaries. The report reviews recent developments and trends in international terrorism that could affect the safety and security of U.S. nuclear weapons research sites and production facilities.

A companion report, *Terrorism in the United States and the Potential Threat to Nuclear Facilities*, R-3351-DOE, by Bruce Hoffman, January 1986, examines the potential threat to nuclear weapons facilities posed by terrorist groups that are active in the United States.

SUMMARY

A review of recent trends in international terrorism shows a steady increase in both the number of terrorist incidents and the casualties resulting from such incidents. This report assesses these trends and their effects on the adversary characterization and threat definition guidelines developed by Rand during the 1970s.

Recent information on the terrorist threat to U.S. nuclear weapons and facilities reveals that the motivation, characteristics, and capabilities of potential adversaries have changed little in the past decade. However, two developments—a dramatic increase in state sponsorship of terrorism (i.e., sponsorship of terrorist groups by foreign governments) and a shift in emphasis within both the American and European anti-nuclear protest movements from *energy* to *weapons*—may necessitate some revisions in nuclear facility defense requirements.

Terrorist actions against nuclear targets over the past 15 years comprise a very small proportion of the terrorist incidents worldwide. Less than 300 of the over 4,000 reported incidents were anti-nuclear in nature,[1] and no attempts have been made to inflict mass casualties through radioactive dispersal. Nevertheless, an attack on a nuclear target is generally perceived as more dangerous than other forms of terrorism, so numbers do not completely represent the potential threat of anti-nuclear terrorism.

The perpetrators of 73 percent of the nuclear incidents that have taken place have been tentatively identified. Hostile employees and economically motivated criminals account for the majority of U.S. nuclear actions, while politically motivated terrorists and extremists were responsible for most of the incidents abroad. In the United States, the major threats have come from individuals who are motivated by personal reasons (such as financial gain or revenge) and who have or desire access to inside information. Hostile employees obviously have access to such information; criminals would like access and probably have it in most of their anti-nuclear crimes. Adversaries of other countries' nuclear facilities, however, act primarily for institutional, governmental, or ideological causes. Anti-nuclear incidents overseas have therefore been more violent and dangerous than those in the United States.

---

[1] "Nuclear incidents" are defined here as actions directed against nuclear targets, either weapons or energy facilities.

No relationship has been found between anti-nuclear protests and nuclear-related crimes, even crimes committed for ideological or political motives. This finding implies that demonstrations are planned to affect decisionmaking rather than to incite violence, but their impact on decisionmakers is uncertain.

Anti-weapons protests in the United States embrace a broader range of issues than do protests abroad. In Europe, the nuclear deployment issue is paramount; in Japan and Australia, the arrivals of ships thought to be carrying nuclear weapons motivate protests; and in New Zealand, the issue of nuclear weapons on U.S. naval vessels has affected government policy. Discussions in the United States tend to center on the arms race and often specifically call for a nuclear freeze.

In recent years, the traditionally strong anti-nuclear movements in Germany and England have lost some of their fervor. At the same time, groups in several other European countries have formed peace movements on the earlier German model, argued for nuclear-free zones, and established "Green" parties. Although protests against nuclear weapons have decreased overall, they reappear each time a country is scheduled to begin deployment of nuclear missiles.

There have been almost no new developments in so-called "taskforce" crimes related to nuclear weapons or facilities since the 1970s.[2] The one exception was the 1980 extortion bombing of Harvey's Casino in Nevada. This incident demonstrated the increasing sophistication of criminals and the potential threat of high-technology adversaries to U.S. nuclear facilities and programs. It also indicated that the use of disguise or deception considerably increases criminals' prospects for success.[3]

The increase of symbolic bombings in the United States, i.e., bombings intended to draw attention to the bombers' cause or existence rather than to destroy a target, suggests that this type of tactic might be used against a nuclear facility. However, visible physical security measures remain a significant deterrent. Although many symbolic bombings are amateurish, a substantial number have recently been committed by more sophisticated groups. Moreover, the shift toward issue-oriented terrorism in this country increases the likelihood that a public crisis or event that involves the nuclear industry (e.g., the Three Mile Island episode) could prompt anti-nuclear terrorist activity. A

---

[2]These are crimes carried out by groups, in which specific responsibilities are delegated to individuals as part of an overall scheme to assault a well-protected target, e.g., a bank vault, an arsenal, or a prison.

[3]Disguises and deception have also been shown to be highly effective in commando raids. See Bruce Hoffman, *Commando Raids: 1946-1983*, The Rand Corporation, N-2316-USDP, October 1985.

nuclear accident with resulting loss of life, for example, could compel a zealous issue-oriented protest group to undertake an active anti-nuclear campaign.

Espionage has been a threat to U.S. nuclear programs since the 1940s, when the Rosenbergs and Karl Fuchs delivered American atomic secrets to the Soviet Union. There have been two major cases of enriched uranium being diverted, possibly to Israel, neither of which has been resolved. More recently, Pakistani and Israeli nationals have been indicted for purchasing nuclear triggering devices. The apparent increase in espionage motivated by personal profit seriously complicates defensive measures. Although multiple safeguards against espionage exist (e.g., requirements for security clearances and compartmentalization of information), the increased value of nuclear information and materials, combined with the possibility of state sponsorship, suggests that increased attention must be paid to espionage safeguards.

The increasing use of terrorist surrogates by foreign governments for a variety of missions demonstrates that elite, commando-type terrorist units are now a distinct possibility. State sponsorship places greater resources at the terrorists' disposal. The sophisticated planning and logistical capabilities, high-level intelligence, technical expertise, and finances available to terrorist organizations imply an increasing likelihood of success for terrorist incidents.

A statistical examination of Rand's database of international terrorist incidents indicates that state-sponsored terrorism is eight times more lethal than non-state-sponsored terrorism. Since state-sponsored terrorists need not worry about alienating perceived constituents, they have few if any constraints against undertaking large-scale attacks. Moreover, because state sponsorship greatly enhances the terrorists' expertise and operational capacity, there is greater likelihood of an assault on a nuclear installation. Terrorists may even offer themselves as mercenaries for such a task.

Although the principal trends in anti-nuclear actions have not changed dramatically since the late 1970s, the increase in state-sponsored terrorist activities and the greater visibility and volatility of anti-nuclear-weapons protests could shape and motivate the future threat to nuclear facilities, and could call for a revision in the defense requirements for those facilities.

ACKNOWLEDGMENTS

This report was a collegial effort in which nearly all the members of Rand's Security and Subnational Conflict Research Program participated. Invaluable contributions were made by Brian Jenkins, the Program Director, and by Konrad Kellen and Jeffrey D. Simon, as well. As she has done so often in the past, Karen Gardela once again provided superlative research assistance. We would also be remiss not to acknowledge Marilyn Yokota, who rescued us from an impending deadline during the preparation of an earlier draft of the report.

The report was greatly improved by the incisive comments and helpful suggestions of George Tanham and John Winkler of the Rand staff, and Donald Lewis of the Aerospace Corporation. Special thanks are also due to Maggie Schumann and the other officials at the Department of Energy's Rocky Flats facility who hosted a visit to the site by two members of the study team.

Finally, the authors' greatest debt is to Janet DeLand, whose skillful editing of an unwieldy manuscript and masterful reconciliation of five competing writing styles vastly improved the final report.

CONTENTS

PREFACE iii

SUMMARY v

ACKNOWLEDGMENTS ix

Section
- I. THE CHANGING THREAT 1
- II. A REVIEW OF THE LITERATURE ON ADVERSARY CHARACTERIZATION AND THREAT DEFINITION . . . 4
- III. NUCLEAR INCIDENTS AND POTENTIALLY THREATENING TERRORIST ACTIVITIES 7
  - Anti-Nuclear Protests 9
  - Symbolic Bombings 12
  - Commando Raids 14
  - Terrorist Assaults 15
  - Espionage 17
- IV. THE THREAT FROM FOREIGN TERRORIST GROUPS 19
- V. CONCLUSION 25

BIBLIOGRAPHY 27

I. THE CHANGING THREAT

Officials in the U.S. Department of Energy (DOE) responsible for nuclear weapons programs have become increasingly concerned over the potential threat to such programs posed by terrorists and other violent political adversaries, economically motivated criminals, hostile employees, foreign agents, ethnic and religious extremists, and mentally unstable individuals. During the 1970s, Rand analyzed the attributes and motivations of potential criminal adversaries to U.S. nuclear programs to determine the types of actions they would find either most or least attractive.[1] Concern has since arisen that the information upon which the analyses are based may be obsolete and the findings may no longer be relevant to the emerging threats of the 1980s.

There has been a steady escalation in both the number of incidents and the casualties caused by terrorists since the early 1980s. The number of terrorist incidents each year has increased by 12 to 15 percent, and the proportion of incidents with multiple fatalities has nearly doubled, from 33 percent in 1982 to 59 percent in 1983. As terrorism has become increasingly lethal, it has also become much more indiscriminate. The number of terrorist attacks directed against ordinary persons—innocent bystanders who happen to be in the wrong place at the wrong time—has increased by 68 percent.[2] State sponsorship of terrorism, i.e., support of terrorist organizations by foreign governments, has increased significantly, providing terrorists with far greater capability than they have had in the past, while eliminating some of their constraints.

This report seeks to determine whether and to what degree these trends may have invalidated the adversary characterization and threat definition guidelines developed at Rand in the 1970s. Our assessment is based on an examination of prior research findings and new evidence concerning the terrorist threat to U.S. nuclear weapons facilities.[3]

---

[1] See Peter deLeon et al., *Attributes of Potential Criminal Adversaries of U.S. Nuclear Programs*, The Rand Corporation, R-2225-SL, February 1978; Gail Bass et al., *Motivations and Possible Actions of Potential Criminal Adversaries of U.S. Nuclear Programs*, The Rand Corporation, R-2554-SL, February 1980; and Gail Bass et al., *The Appeal of Nuclear Crimes to the Spectrum of Potential Adversaries*, The Rand Corporation, R-2803-SL, February 1982.

[2] Bonnie Cordes et al., *Trends in International Terrorism, 1982 and 1983*, The Rand Corporation, R-3183-SL, August 1984, p. 5.

[3] Nuclear weapons facilities are defined here as plants and research laboratories in the United States that are connected with nuclear weapons development and production.

The key problem in assessing the terrorist threat to nuclear programs is the lack of empirical data. Because there have been few actual incidents against nuclear facilities, it is necessary to rely on analogs.[4] However, there is more evidence available today than there was in the 1970s. A 1978 Rand study of attributes was based on 45 possibly analogous crimes,[5] whereas today, the database of such crimes contains 121 incidents. Data were available on 48 terrorist assaults on embassies in 1980, while the number has now increased to 184.[6] There are now over 150 commando raids in the Rand database, twice as many as there were seven years ago. One hundred "symbolic bombings"[7] were available for analysis in the 1978 study; the database now contains 212. Between 1968 and 1975, data were collected on 288 actions directed against nuclear targets (240 of them were threats); the database now includes 292 actual incidents.[8]

It therefore seems imperative to ask whether the threat assessments calculated from earlier data are still relevant. The earlier assessments may still be pertinent and hence usable, but conditions have changed sufficiently since the mid-1970s that the trends should be examined and their possible effects taken into account. The increase in state-supported terrorism and a shift of emphasis within both the American and European anti-nuclear movements from nuclear energy to nuclear weapons will almost certainly have a significant effect on the terrorist threat to nuclear facilities.

The remainder of this report comprises three main parts: Section II reviews the recent literature pertaining to adversary characterization and threat definition. Section III examines and summarizes recent trends and developments in international terrorism to determine how

---

They include, but are not limited to, the Lawrence Livermore, Los Alamos, and Sandia (Albuquerque) research laboratories; the weapons production facilities at Rocky Flats, Pantex, Oak Ridge (Y-12), Savannah River, Kansas City, and Dayton; and the Nevada Test Site.

[4]The analogs comprise several categories of conventional crimes and political violence that are similar in their aims and operations to possible crimes involving nuclear weapons facilities or nuclear material. Study of these analogs may provide knowledge and insights into the capabilities and *modus operandi* of potential adversaries to nuclear programs, as well as evidence about the methods by which objectives such as theft, sabotage, or extortion might be achieved. (See deLeon et al., op. cit.)

[5]R. N. Reinstedt and Judith Westbury, *Major Crimes as Analogs to Potential Threats to Nuclear Facilities and Programs,* The Rand Corporation, N-1498-SL, April 1980.

[6]See Brian M. Jenkins, *Embassies Under Siege: A Review of 48 Embassy Takeovers, 1971-1980,* The Rand Corporation, R-2651-RC, January 1981.

[7]I.e., bombings used to draw attention to the terrorists' cause or existence, rather than to destroy assets.

[8]A Rand database of industrial sabotage was created specifically for the study reported in deLeon et al., op. cit., and has not been updated.

the adversary characterization and threat definition may have changed. Section IV examines foreign terrorist groups that might undertake operations in the United States. Finally, Section V presents policy conclusions derived from the study.

II. A REVIEW OF THE LITERATURE ON ADVERSARY CHARACTERIZATION AND THREAT DEFINITION

Earlier studies of the terrorist threat to nuclear weapons facilities examined the capabilities and intentions of a variety of adversarial groups. Capabilities include the size of the groups, their equipment (weapons, transportation, munitions, etc.), their skill and training, their planning capacities, and their resolve.[1] At least some of these factors can be quantified, and objective conclusions can be drawn. The delineation of intentions is much more subjective.[2] Because there have been very few nuclear-related terrorist incidents, the database on such activities is inadequate to enable reliable inferences to be drawn. Therefore, analogous criminal activities, such as so-called "task-force" crimes, have been studied to determine what sorts of capabilities well-organized and directed criminal groups could assemble or would be likely to assemble if they opted to target and attack a nuclear facility.

Task-force crimes are organized efforts in which specific responsibilities are delegated to each person involved, as part of an overall scheme to assault a well-protected target.[3] Task-force criminals almost always use surreptitious means, attempting to draw as little attention to themselves as possible, and this distinguishes them from their terrorist counterparts, whose major goal is often publicity. Nevertheless, task-force crimes appear to be appropriate analogs to potential anti-nuclear attacks because both types of operation require careful planning and execution, as well as specialized skills. A 1978 Rand study of 45 task-force crimes found that:

1. Almost all of the crimes examined were successful. (It must be noted, however, that successful crimes are more widely reported than failures, and thus the actual proportion of failures is not known.)
2. Task-force criminals engage in long periods of surveillance and reconnaissance.
3. Violence is usually kept to a minimum; however, where weapons are necessary (e.g., in armed robberies), they are used

---
[1] deLeon et al., op. cit.
[2] Bass et al., *Motivations and Possible Actions*, op. cit.
[3] deLeon et al., op. cit., p. 11.

in large numbers to demonstrate overwhelming firepower and thereby discourage resistance.
4. Task-force criminals show little inclination to risk capture or death, seeking to avoid rather than overpower guards. Significantly, politically motivated adversaries are willing to assume greater risks and come prepared to fight.[4]
5. Insider help is often essential in task-force crimes.
6. All of the crimes in which impersonation was used were successful.
7. Few of the crimes involved more than seven perpetrators.

A follow-up study of 121 crimes that were regarded as potentially relevant to nuclear crimes found that:

1. The higher the potential economic gain of the crime, the more persons are involved and the more likely it is that insiders will be used.
2. The use of insiders increases the risk of apprehension.
3. A large number of major thefts occur while the targeted assets are in transit.
4. Crimes of coercion most often involve an insider having authority and access, and are usually successful.
5. Deception greatly enhances the chances of success for an operation.

Extortion attempts are also possible analogs for anti-nuclear actions. For example, a desk-sized box covered with plastic was delivered to the executive suite of Harvey's Casino in Stateline, Nevada, in August 1980. A three-page extortion note sent to the Casino warned against attempting to move the box, which was said to contain a bomb that would detonate at the slightest movement. Experts from the DOE, the FBI, and the Army's Explosives Ordnance Disposal Team examined the device and found it to be extremely sophisticated. X-rays showed that it contained 1,100 pounds of explosives. Attempts to disarm the bomb failed, and it exploded, causing $12 million worth of damage to the Casino. This incident demonstrated the increasing sophistication of criminals, including potential "high-tech" adversaries to U.S. nuclear facilities and programs.

Other analogs such as commando raids and terrorist assaults have been used to derive a first approximation of the potential that could be

---

[4]For example, a group of 12 terrorists held up a Brinks armored car in Nyack, New York, on October 20, 1981, to acquire operating funds for their group. In the course of the holdup, they killed two police officers and wounded one; four of the terrorists were arrested.

mounted against nuclear facilities. Based on these analogs, "typical" threats have been identified. Concerns regarding the possibilities of inside collaboration have now been included, slightly expanding the threat calculus. It is estimated that an attack on a nuclear facility would probably involve 6 or 7 outside, well-armed, dedicated attackers and 1 or 2 inside collaborators.[5]

It must be emphasized that all the numbers given here were derived from a database that included very few nuclear incidents. The analog approach and findings, however, have been generally accepted in the research and policy communities,[6] and these estimates have been widely used as the baseline against which threat requirements can be set.[7]

Very few threat analyses have been performed since the 1978 Rand work was completed. The most recent published works on nuclear program safeguards have been oriented toward either deterring potential adversaries[8] or preventing them from achieving their objectives once an attack has been initiated.[9] Current safeguards research at Los Alamos National Laboratories focuses on time as the critical defense variable, on the assumption that the longer the adversary's progress can be delayed, the greater are the chances of defeating his objectives. Recent emphasis has been on heavier doors and more sophisticated lock mechanisms. No significant revision has been made of the threat assessment estimates or methodologies defined in the late 1970s.

---

[5]These numbers were cited in a report published by the U.S. Congress, Office of Technology Assessment, *Nuclear Proliferation and Safeguards*, Washington, D.C.: U.S. Government Printing Office, 1976; also New York: Praeger, 1977.

[6]E.g., John B. Steward, Jr., et al., *Generic Adversary Characteristics: Summary Report*, U.S. Nuclear Regulatory Commission, NUREG-0459, Washington, D.C., March 1979; N. E. Wagner, *A Survey of Threat Studies Relating to the Nuclear Power Industry*, Sandia Laboratories, August 1977.

[7]Michael K. Pilgrim and R. William Mengel, *Handbook for Development of Deterrent Strategies*, Department of Energy, September 1981; also, Craig W. Kirkwood and Stephen M. Pollock, *Methodology for Characterizing Potential Adversaries of Nuclear Safeguards Systems*, Woodward-Clyde, San Francisco, 1978.

[8]E.g., Pilgrim and Mengel, op. cit.

[9]See J. C. Scarborough and C. A. Russell, "Nuclear Plant Security in the 1980s-90s," paper delivered at the American Nuclear Society, Atlanta, Georgia, June 1979.

III. NUCLEAR INCIDENTS AND POTENTIALLY THREATENING TERRORIST ACTIVITIES

This section reviews and analyzes the actions that have been directed against nuclear targets, i.e., the "nuclear incidents" to date, and other terrorist activities that pose a potential threat to nuclear facilities. The database for this analysis was compiled from public domain sources, such as trade journals and newspaper accounts, and there is no guarantee that *all* anti-nuclear incidents are included. Indeed, there were no serious, illegal actions against any U.S. nuclear facility or program reported in 1983 or 1984. There appears to be a significant decline in anti-nuclear attacks worldwide, but this should not lead policymakers into a false sense of security. Nor does it necessarily justify a reduction in nuclear security measures or policies. The potential nuclear adversary's means and goals can change so suddenly that no prematurely optimistic conclusions are warranted. Finally, it would be inappropriate to assign statistical significance to the findings reported here. Not only is there no assurance that all anti-nuclear activities are reflected in the data, the sample size is too small to produce reliably valid results. Nevertheless, the trends revealed may prove illustrative for nuclear security planners.

Table 1 shows the numbers of anti-nuclear incidents that occurred in the United States and abroad between 1970 and 1984, by mission objective. Of the more than 4,000 terrorist incidents that took place in those years, less than 300 (around 7 percent) were anti-nuclear.[1] Attacks on nuclear targets, however, are generally perceived as more dangerous than other forms of terrorism, so raw numbers do not completely reflect the perceived threat.

Overseas adversaries of nuclear facilities apparently were slow to recognize nuclear plants as valuable targets of opportunity (only four incidents occurred abroad in 1970–74), but that situation had changed dramatically by the end of the 1970s. Two-thirds of all recorded anti-nuclear actions in the 1980s occurred outside the United States.

Moreover, non-U.S. nuclear adversaries were more violent, as reflected in the greater number of destructive and casualty-causing incidents. Destruction levels of U.S. anti-nuclear actions did, however,

---

[1]Data from the Rand Chronology of International Terrorism, which records international terrorist incidents from 1968 to the present.

Table 1

ANTI-NUCLEAR INCIDENTS, 1970–84, BY MISSION OBJECTIVE

Mission	1970–74	1975–79	1980–84	Total
U.S. Incidents				
Casualties	0	0	2	2
Seizure	0	8	6	14
Destruction	6	10	26	42
Disruption	12	23	14	49
Total U.S.	18	41	48	107
Non-U.S. Incidents				
Casualties	1	3	9	13
Seizure	1	9	13	23
Destruction	0	61	53	114
Disruption	2	12	21	35
Total non-U.S.	4	85	96	185
TOTALS	22	126	144	292

increase in 1980–82, rising to 26 reported cases, compared with 10 for 1975–79.

Eight of the nine casualty operations directed at non-U.S. nuclear personnel were aimed at carefully selected individuals closely associated with the nuclear industry.[2] There were no reported casualty incidents abroad in 1983–84, and to date there have been no actions aimed at producing mass casualties through the release of radioactivity.

The perpetrators of 214 of the 292 anti-nuclear incidents (73 percent) have been tentatively categorized, and the results are shown in Table 2. Hostile employees and criminals perpetrated the majority of U.S. nuclear actions, while foreign facilities were most threatened by terrorists and extremists.[3] The major threat to U.S. facilities has come from individuals acting for personal reasons (e.g., financial gain or revenge) and having access to inside information.[4] The threat overseas has come mainly from violent adversaries acting for ideological causes.

---

[2]In the ninth incident, three Frenchmen known to favor a nuclear project were mailed radioactive pellets.

[3]This is not particularly surprising, since terrorists are more active abroad than in the United States. The high proportion of hostile employees among perpetrators of U.S. anti-nuclear actions may also be due simply to more complete reporting of such incidents in the U.S. media.

[4]This trend is supported by the recent spate of arrests for national security violations in the United States. (See Rudy Abramson and Ronald J. Ostrow, "Money Seen as Motivating Today's Spies," *Los Angeles Times*, June 7, 1985, Sec. I, pp. 1, 14.)

Table 2

ANTI-NUCLEAR ADVERSARIES, 1970–84

Adversary Type	U.S.	Overseas
Criminal	20	13
Dissident-protector	7	15
Extremist	16	40
Foreign agent	2	11
Hostile employee	23	2
Military-mercenary	0	5
Terrorist	4	56
Totals	72	142

This finding also supports the observation that mission and tactical patterns overseas have been more violent and dangerous than those in the United States.

ANTI-NUCLEAR PROTESTS[5]

Anti-nuclear protests have generally focused on either nuclear energy or nuclear weapons.[6] Energy protests are intended to prevent or disrupt the construction and licensing of nuclear power plants, while weapons protests are generally aimed at the arms race and concern such events as the deployment of cruise and Pershing missiles and the docking of nuclear-powered aircraft carriers.

Anti-nuclear energy protests in the United States peaked in 1979, and those abroad peaked about a year later. As the energy issue waned, anti-nuclear weapons protests began to increase in frequency, reaching their highest point in 1983.[7] Since 1983, anti-nuclear weapons protests have continued, especially abroad, but with far less frequency and intensity. The energy issue has seen no significant revival since its decline in 1980. These trends are summarized in Table 3.

---

[5]This discussion is based largely on data from Rand chronologies of anti-nuclear energy and anti-nuclear weapons protests. For a detailed study of this subject see Victoria L. Daubert and Sue Ellen Moran, *Origins, Goals, and Tactics of the U.S. Anti-Nuclear Protest Movement*, The Rand Corporation, N-2192-SL, March 1985.

[6]While many protesters have combined the two, the dichotomy is usually observed; see, for instance, Hazel Gandet Erskine, "The Polls: Atomic Weapons and Nuclear Energy," *Public Opinion Quarterly*, Vol. 27, No. 2, Summer 1963.

[7]Fox Butterfield, "Anatomy of the Nuclear Protest," *The New York Times Magazine*, July 11, 1984.

Table 3

ANTI-NUCLEAR ENERGY AND WEAPONS PROTESTS, 1977–84

	U.S. Protests		Non-U.S. Protests	
Year	Anti-Energy	Anti-Weapons	Anti-Energy	Anti-Weapons
1977	4	5	..	..
1978	24	21	..	..
1979	31	9	..	..
1980	10	4	13	2
1981	7	8	12	15
1982	9	11	12	10
1983	9	185	5	97
1984	1	11	0	50

Much of the protest activity of 1983 occurred in the months preceding the deployment of the first intermediate-range nuclear force (INF) missiles in Europe.[8] In the United States, 140 anti-nuclear weapons rallies took place on one weekend (October 24–25, 1983). Overseas, 60 of the year's 97 anti-nuclear weapons incidents took place between September and December.

Anti-nuclear protests take the form of demonstrations, marches, intrusions, vandalism, symbolic protests, or blockades. The most common tactic worldwide is large public demonstrations. The second most common tactic in the United States is intrusion, while marches are the second most popular tactic overseas.

There appears to be no relationship between protest actions and incidents of nuclear-related crime. Nuclear-related crime has not risen when the number of protests has increased, not even nuclear crimes committed for ideological or political motives. Protest demonstrations are primarily intended to affect decisionmaking at critical times, when outcomes are still uncertain or subject to change. For example, a two-week protest at the Diablo Canyon nuclear facility in California in September 1981 was mounted in an effort to prevent the loading of nuclear fuel into the reactor for testing. The demonstration was unsuccessful, and energy protests in the United States all but disap-

---

[8]The situation is examined in Manfred Worner, "The 'Peace Movement' and NATO: An Alternative View from Bonn," *Strategic Review*, Vol. 10, No. 1, Winter 1982, pp. 15–21; and Jeffrey Bontwell, "Politics and the Peace Movement in Western Germany," *International Security*, Vol. 7, No. 4, Spring 1983, pp. 72–91.

peared after that. Likewise, once the INF deployment had commenced, anti-nuclear weapons protest activity in Europe began to decline.[9]

Anti-nuclear weapons protests in the United States tend to embrace a broader range of issues than do protests abroad. The issues raised by the American protesters generally become part of a larger discussion about the need for the arms race and the dangers of nuclear exchange, as reflected in the multiple and occasionally disparate objectives of the American nuclear-freeze movement of the early 1980s.[10] In Europe, the deployment issue is paramount, while in Japan and Australia, most protests occur in response to the arrivals of nuclear-powered aircraft carriers.

Protests abroad usually last longer than those in the United States. The German nuclear plant at Whyl was occupied by protesters for a full year in 1975, while the two-week-long protests at Diablo Canyon in 1977 and 1981 were long by U.S. standards. The longest weapons protest in the United States lasted three days, while the longest abroad lasted four days. (These statistics do not include encampment protests, which are characterized by the establishment of temporary living quarters on or near the premises.) The longer protests abroad may reflect a more sustained public interest in anti-nuclear issues there.

In 1984 and 1985, the traditionally strong anti-nuclear movements in Germany and England began to lose some of their fervor.[11] At the same time, groups in several other European countries, including the Scandinavian nations and Iceland, have formed German-style peace movements, argued for nuclear-free zones, and established "Green" parties. The clergy—most notably, the American and French Catholic bishops and Pope John Paul II—have continued to voice their concerns about nuclear weapons and their support of a freeze.[12]

As part of the anti-nuclear protest activity, nuclear-free zones have been established in several American and foreign communities, students at Brown University proposed the stockpiling of suicide pills for

---

[9]The effectiveness of anti-nuclear weapons protests in influencing national security policy is questioned in Bernard M. Kraemer et al., "Attitudes Towards Nuclear Weapons and Nuclear War: 1945–1982," *Journal of Social Issues*, Vol. 39, No. 1, 1983.

[10]See Peter deLeon, "Freeze: The Literature of the Nuclear Weapons Debate," *Journal of Conflict Resolution*, Vol. 27, No. 1, March 1983, pp. 181–189; and Tom R. Tyler and Kathleen M. McGraw, "The Threat of Nuclear War: Risk Interpretations and Behavioral Responses," *Journal of Social Issues*, Vol. 39, No. 1, 1983, pp. 25–40.

[11]These traditions are examined by Dorothy Nelkin and Michael Pollack, *The Atom Besieged*, Cambridge, Massachusetts: The MIT Press, 1982.

[12]Bruce M. Russett, "Ethical Dilemmas of Nuclear Deterrence," *International Security*, Vol. 8, No. 4, Spring 1984, pp. 36–54, describes the deliberations that preceded a Pastoral Letter of the U.S. Catholic Bishops. Also see *The Church and the Bomb: Nuclear Weapons and Christian Conscience*, Report of a Working Party under the Chairmanship of the Bishop of Salisbury, London: Hodder & Stoughton, 1982.

use in the event of a nuclear attack, and portrayals of nuclear holocausts (e.g., *The Day After* and *Testament*) have had international showings.[13] Although anti-nuclear weapons protests have decreased significantly, they reappear each time a country is asked to implement its decision to deploy medium-range missiles.

The decline in anti-nuclear protests in the United States has been accompanied by an increased visibility and public recognition of the issues. Incidents such as the accident at Three Mile Island and the debate over nuclear weapons and the arms race have fueled this higher visibility, as nuclear matters have increasingly entered the political arena.[14] It is difficult to predict what effect this heightened visibility will have on the security of U.S. nuclear facilities, but it is apparent that such publicity could form larger anti-nuclear constituencies than might otherwise exist. This development could contribute, probably indirectly, to a more hostile threat environment.

SYMBOLIC BOMBINGS

Symbolic bombings, i.e., deliberate acts of violence calculated to express a grievance or make a political statement, are intended to draw attention to a terrorist cause or to a group's existence, rather than to destroy targets. Efforts are usually made to avoid victims, although targets may be damaged intentionally. (Symbolic bombings claimed only one life between 1976 and 1984, although more than 60 people were injured in such attacks.)

In 1978, data were available on 110 symbolic bombings that occurred in the United States between 1965 and 1976.[15] The number nearly doubled in the next decade, rising to 212. This rise parallels the worldwide increase in terrorist activity, and it also indicates that bombings have gained currency in this country as a means of political expression.

In the past decade, terrorism in the United States has become more issue-oriented. The New World Liberation Front, for example, carried out an attack against a utility company in 1977 in the name of an elderly man who froze to death when the electric company turned off his power because of an unpaid $18 bill. The group also bombed

---

[13]See L. Bruce van Voorst, "The Critical Masses," *Foreign Policy*, No. 48, Fall 1982, pp. 82–93.

[14]E.g., "The Freeze Issue Has Reagan on the Spot," *Business Week*, May 16, 1983, p. 16; and Daniel Yankelovich and John Doble, "Nuclear Weapons and the U.S.S.R.: The Public Mood," *Foreign Affairs*, Vol. 3, No. 1, Fall 1984, pp. 33–46.

[15]deLeon et al., op. cit.

pylons in an attempt to force utilities to provide free electricity for senior citizens.

During 1984, symbolic bombings by groups protesting legalized abortion also increased. Groups calling themselves the Army of God, God's Army, and the Army of the Living God bombed abortion clinics both to attract attention to their cause and to close down the clinics.

The most frequent targets of symbolic bombings are commercial organizations, which have accounted for 25 percent of the recorded attacks. Government targets have declined in popularity, accounting for less than 10 percent of the attacks, while attacks against diplomatic targets comprised nearly 25 percent of all symbolic bombings between 1976 and 1984. Foreign airlines offices were also frequently targeted. The shift from American to foreign targets, however, does not seem significant for U.S. nuclear facility security unless nuclear energy becomes an active public issue.

Symbolic bombings have been carried out by Iranian, Taiwanese, Croatian, anti-Cuban, Puerto Rican, Armenian, Jewish, and left-wing, issue-oriented groups, some of which have demonstrated willingness and capabilities for deadlier, more sophisticated operations. Some bombings, such as the multiple bombings by a Puerto Rican group in New York City on New Year's Eve 1983, have reflected elaborate planning. But many appear to be the work of nonprofessionals or new recruits. The choice of target still appears to rest heavily on proximity and convenience.

New indigenous U.S. groups have also emerged, including the Red Guerrilla Resistance, the United Freedom Fighters, the United Freedom Front, and the Armed Resistance Unit. Each group has its own agenda and aims, but few of the terrorists are so wedded to a specific cause that they might not shift to other volatile public issues.

The increase in symbolic bombing activity in the United States may indicate a growing likelihood of such action being taken against a nuclear facility. However, visible physical security measures at such targets appear to be a significant deterrent. The shift toward issue-oriented terrorism may also increase the likelihood that a nuclear crisis or event could encourage anti-nuclear terrorist activity. A nuclear facility accident that causes some loss of life, for instance, could inspire a zealous, issue-oriented group to embark on an emotional and violent anti-nuclear campaign.

COMMANDO RAIDS

Commando raids are included in the analog database because they exemplify the capabilities that are needed to overcome a well-defended target such as a guarded nuclear facility. Moreover, commando-type operations represent the only documented *military* or *paramilitary* assaults against such targets. Commando raids thus provide some insights into the strategies that seem most effective for attacking nuclear facilities.[16]

Three elements (also common to conventional military operations) have been found to determine the success or failure of a commando mission: (1) accurate intelligence, (2) careful planning, and (3) surprise. Seventy-six percent of the commando or commando-type raids examined in the 1978 Rand study were successful. Well-planned and well-executed assaults, characterized by imagination on the part of the attacker and the advantage of surprise, almost always succeed, even in the face of well-armed, trained defenders and formidable physical barriers.[17]

Subsequent analysis of 100 additional commando raids supported these conclusions.[18] These included raids by elite, national armed forces, as well as raids by irregular forces (e.g., guerrilla bands, small terrorist groups, and individuals) that evinced similar skills, planning, sophistication, and dedication.[19] The success rate achieved by assaults in the more recent period, 77 percent, was almost the same as that achieved earlier. The critical elements identified in the earlier study were shown to be still valid. For example, all raids in which surprise, disguise, or deception were used were successful.

Although the objectives of commando operations vary greatly (for example, from destruction or sabotage missions to rescues, from individual assassinations to wholesale murder), they are all carried out by small groups, i.e., less than 200 men, and sometimes by only one or two men. Their combination of stealth, discipline, and firepower mark commando activities as potentially successful, even against resolute and trained defenses.

There is some possibility that a U.S. nuclear installation could be subjected to a commando-type attack by a well-financed and well-led

---

[16]Ibid., p. 18.
[17]Ibid., p. 20.
[18]Bruce Hoffman, *Commando Raids: 1946-1983*, The Rand Corporation, N-2316-USDP, November 1985.
[19]Some of these incidents could also be categorized as "terrorist assaults" (described below).

terrorist organization.[20] The prospect of such an organization was only hypothesized a decade ago, but recent events have demonstrated that such terrorist organizations are now a reality. Although none has ever been deployed against a nuclear facility, the vulnerability of nuclear power facilities to terrorist attacks and the inadequacy of current defensive measures are well-documented.[21]

Indian Prime Minister Rajiv Gandhi has charged that Sikh extremists have, in fact, targeted Indian nuclear power stations.[22] And the Israeli destruction of the Iraqi nuclear reactor at Osirak in June 1981 underscores the potential of state-sponsored actions against nuclear facilities.[23]

As state sponsorship of terrorism places greater resources in the hands of terrorists, levels of terrorist planning and logistical capabilities, intelligence, technical expertise, finances, and sophistication higher than those evidenced in the successful commando raids of the past can be expected.

TERRORIST ASSAULTS

Terrorist assaults are particularly relevant as analogs for possible nuclear-related actions in that they embody many of the characteristics an adversarial force might employ in an attack against a nuclear facility. Terrorists are generally highly motivated and willing to assume great risks. In the terrorist incidents recorded between 1968 and 1974, the perpetrators sought out targets that were highly visible (ensuring maximum publicity) and to which they were likely to succeed in gaining entry. At that time, there appeared to be little likelihood that terrorists would attempt to seize nuclear material by attacking a well-protected nuclear facility.[24] However, with the increase in state sponsorship, terrorism is geared less to obtaining publicity than to carrying

---

[20]Ibid, p. 18.

[21]See Bennett Ramberg, *An Unrecognized Military Peril*, Berkeley: University of California Press, 1984.

[22]Rone Tempest, "Gandhi Says FBI Should Have Told Him Sooner of Terrorist Death Plot," *Los Angeles Times*, June 5, 1985, Sec. I, p. 5.

[23]The Israeli actions are analyzed by Amos Perlmutter, "The Israeli Raid on Iraq: A New Proliferation Landscape," *Strategic Review*, Vol. 10, No. 1, Winter 1982, pp. 34–43. See also Don Oberdorfer, "Pakistan Concerned About Attack on Atomic Plants," *Washington Post*, October 12, 1984, p.44A; and "Hindu-Jew 'Conspiracy' Prepares Attack on Atomic Installation," *Nawa-I-Waqt*, LaHore, editorial, September 16, 1984, p. 2 (JPRS-NEA-84-160, October 26, 1984).

[24]deLeon et al., op. cit., p. xiii.

out government policy and bringing pressure to bear on the sponsor's opponents.

The state-sponsored terrorist does not have to be a rabid ideologue or a nationalist/ethnic or religious zealot, but can be an independent "gun-for-hire," available for the right price.[25] Moreover, since 1980, international terrorist incidents have grown at a rate of approximately 30 percent per year, and the numbers of fatalities caused by terrorist attacks have increased alarmingly.

A review of the 184 post-1980 terrorist attacks, however, shows that terrorist tactics have changed little. Bombings still account for over half the total number of incidents and the weaponry employed by terrorists remains relatively constant. There is no firm evidence that terrorists are on the verge of obtaining nuclear weapons or using nuclear, biological, or chemical dispersal devices.

There has been increased terrorist use of car and truck bombs, related in part to the decline of barricade-and-hostage situations since the 1970s. As security at embassies and other lucrative targets has increased, terrorists have been forced to devise new means and methods of staging operations to gain their objectives. Between 1971 and 1980, the likelihood of governments acceding to terrorists' demands dropped by nearly 50 percent. Furthermore, by 1980, the inclination of governments to use force rather than concessions to end a barricade-and-hostage situation resulted in the capture or death of half the terrorists involved in such incidents.[26]

As embassies and government offices have become more difficult to penetrate, terrorists have turned to the kidnapping and assassination of individual diplomats and government officials outside of the government compound. If senior diplomats are too well protected, minor officials can be seized or murdered instead. If heightened security and detection methods prevent the placing of explosives inside an embassy, explosives-laden vehicles can be crashed into the compound or driveway. Although terrorists have rarely assaulted facilities where there was a high probability that they might be defeated before they gained entry, they have continually evolved new means of attacking hardened targets, which implies that the threat to well-guarded facilities still exists.

---

[25]The shadowy Islamic Jihad, which is presently active in Lebanon and has taken credit for the bombing of American, French, and Israeli targets in that country, is believed to be closely linked to, if not supported by, Syria and Iran. Islamic Jihad is probably not a group at all, but an ad hoc collection of persons operating at the behest of these two governments.

[26]Jenkins, op. cit.

Terrorists could take advantage of the fact that even an unsuccessful attempt at stealing a nuclear weapon would probably produce highly unsettling effects. The disaster of having a nuclear weapon in hands other than those of a recognized government could cause worldwide alarm. Whereas ten years ago, the principal concern was that terrorists might use a nuclear device for blackmail or detonation, concern has now shifted to whether terrorists might undertake some nuclear-related action to create a popular disturbance. Such a disturbance would allow opponents of current policies to garner support from a population that is seriously worried about nuclear security.

The constraints that existed ten years ago against terrorist use of a nuclear device still pertain, although they are perhaps somewhat diminished. However, a new situation with a wide range of potential policy effects now exists. Where a disturbance at a nuclear depot or a foiled attempt to steal a nuclear weapon would have caused only consternation ten years ago, it could now have serious policy repercussions. Because terrorists recognize this, the threat to nuclear facilities has inevitably increased.

The increasing trend toward state sponsorship of terrorism might prompt states desiring their own nuclear capability to use terrorist surrogates to seize nuclear material. Thus, the proliferation of nuclear weapons could also produce a demand for state-sponsored assaults against nuclear facilities.[27]

ESPIONAGE

Espionage represents a distinct threat to nuclear facilities in that a successful agent can illegally gain considerable information or materials. Because espionage acts often go undetected, there are not enough documented cases to build a statistically useful database for analysis; but the tradition of spying and covert theft regarding nuclear programs goes back to the 1940s, when the Rosenbergs and Klaus Fuchs passed American atomic secrets to Soviet agents.

More recently, there have been two cases of apparent diversion of nuclear materials to foreign nations. In November 1968, the West German freighter *Scheersberg,* loaded with 200 metric tons of uranium oxide, left Antwerp, bound for Genoa. Sixteen days later, with no noted docking, it arrived in Turkey minus its radioactive cargo. Although no conclusive proof exists, it is commonly thought that the

---

[27]The growing fear of nuclear proliferation is discussed in a report by Leonard R. Spector which is summarized in Fred Hiatt, "Edging Toward Nuclear Doom: Several Nations Reported Moving Toward the Bomb," *Washington Post,* October 31, 1984.

uranium oxide was diverted into Israeli hands.[28] The second case involved the loss and suspected diversion of up to 500 pounds of highly enriched uranium from the now-defunct Nuclear Materials and Equipment Corporation (NUMEC) facility near Apollo, Pennsylvania. Investigations into the amount and destination of the diversion began in 1965 and came to light in the late 1970s. Although, again, there is no concrete evidence, Israel is the suspected culprit;[29] however, some have claimed that the "loss" was in fact an error in NUMEC's accounting.[30]

Indictments have recently been handed up regarding the illegal procurement by foreign agents of devices that could be used in the design and production of nuclear weapons. Federal agents arrested a Pakistani for attempting to smuggle 50 krytrons (timing devices used to trigger nuclear explosions) out of Houston.[31] Israel has admitted purchasing U.S. krytrons, but has denied any intention to use the devices for nuclear purposes or to send them to other countries.[32]

In conjunction with recently revealed national security violations in the United States, these cases of nuclear espionage portend a possible and very severe threat to U.S. nuclear facilities. The newly evident motivation of greed in a crime traditionally motivated by ideology has also complicated defense requirements.[33]

---

[28] Robert Gillette, "200 Tons of Uranium Lost; Israel May Have It," *Los Angeles Times*, April 29, 1977, pp. 1, 21; and David Burham, "1968 Mystery of a Vanished Ship: Did Its Uranium End Up in Israel?" *The New York Times*, April 29, 1977, pp. A1, A7.

[29] See David Burnham, "House Aide Tells of Suspicion U.S. Uranium Was Stolen Ten Years Ago," *The New York Times*, August 9, 1977; and David Burnham, "U.S. Agencies Suspected Missing Uranium Went to Israel for Arms," *The New York Times*, November 6, 1977.

[30] David Burnham, "The Case of the Missing Uranium," *The Atlantic Monthly*, Vol. 243, No. 4, April 1979, pp. 78–82.

[31] Seymour M. Hersh, "A Pakistani Tried to Send Trigger for A-Bomb Home," *The New York Times*, February 25, 1985, pp. 1, 6.

[32] John M. Goshko, "Israel Got U.S.-Made Devices," *Washington Post*, April 14, 1985, p. A1; and John M. Goshko, "L.A. Man Indicted in Export of Potential Nuclear Bomb Component to Israel," *Washington Post*, May 17, 1985, p. A27.

[33] Joel Brinkley, "Methods and Aims Point to a New Breed of Spy," *The New York Times*, June 9, 1985, Sec. I, pp. 1, 20.

IV. THE THREAT FROM FOREIGN TERRORIST GROUPS

Rand maintains an extensive database on currently active terrorist groups, which includes information on the known attributes of each group, e.g., the number of members in a group, the group's preferred tactics, and whether it has received assistance from other groups. Of course, information is not available on every attribute for every group, and missing information may, in some cases, be significant.

To help determine the threat to U.S. nuclear programs posed by organized terrorist groups outside the United States, we examined the database entries for the organizations listed in Table 4. Analysis of data on the motivation, resources, and capabilities of groups indicates with some reliability which groups might be more likely than others to attack a nuclear facility in the United States.

Our analysis addressed the following questions:

1. Does a particular terrorist group represent a threat to the United States? Is it likely to attack U.S. citizens or facilities? Is it likely to carry out operations within the United States?
2. Has the group demonstrated the ability to operate outside of its immediate geographic location? To what extent?
3. What is the level of technical sophistication of the group? What resources and capabilities does the group have for carrying out a terrorist operation?
4. Does any particular group pose a threat to U.S. nuclear programs or installations?

We first identified those groups that have attacked U.S. targets in the past (see Table 5). None has thus far targeted American energy installations, although some have attacked installations belonging to other countries. (Palestinian groups made a concerted effort to disrupt Middle Eastern oil pipeline operations during the 1970s, and the Islamic Jihad bombed an electrical substation in Kuwait in December 1983.)

Very few of the groups we examined have operated outside their home country, however, so we eliminated all those that have carried out no international attacks, on the assumption that they would be unlikely to carry out an operation in the United States. Only five groups of terrorists that have attacked American targets remained: the Armenian Secret Army for the Liberation of Armenia (ASALA), the

Table 4

ACTIVE FOREIGN TERRORIST GROUPS

Group	Nationality
Armenian Secret Army for the Liberation of Armenia (ASALA)	Armenian
Justice Commandos for the Armenian Genocide (JCAG)	Armenian
Movement of the Revolutionary Left (MIR)	Chilean
Movement of April 19 (M-19)	Colombian
Revolutionary Armed Forces of Colombia	Colombian
Action Directe (AD)	French
Red Army Faction (RAF)	German
Guerrilla Army of the Poor (EGP)	Guatemalan
Guatemalan Labor Party (PGT)	Guatemalan
Rebel Armed Forces of Guatemala (FAR)	Guatemalan
Organization of the People in Arms (ORPA)	Guatemalan
Provisional Irish Republican Army (PIRA)	Irish
Irish National Liberation Army (INLA)	Irish
Red Brigades (BR)	Italian
Prima Linea (PL)	Italian
Japanese Red Army	Japanese
Libyan agents	Libyan
Al Fatah	Palestinian
As-Sa'iqa	Palestinian
Black June	Palestinian
Popular Front for the Liberation of Palestine (PFLP)	Palestinian
Popular Front for the Liberation of Palestine–General Command (PFLP-GC)	Palestinian
Democratic Front for the Liberation of Palestine (DFLP)	Palestinian
Sendero Luminoso (Shining Path)	Peruvian
Moro National Liberation Front (MNLF)	Philippine
African National Congress (ANC)	South African
ETA (Basque Homeland and Liberty)	Spanish
Pattani United Liberation Organization (PULO)	Thai
Dev Sol	Turkish
Dev Yol	Turkish
Marxist-Leninist Armed Propaganda Unit (MLAPU)	Turkish
Islamic Jihad	Islamic

Table 5

FOREIGN TERRORIST GROUPS THAT HAVE ATTACKED AMERICAN TARGETS

Group	Tactic	Target
Action Directe	Attacks on installations Bombings Shootings	Diplomatic Business
Armenian Secret Army for the Liberation of Armenia	Bombings	Airlines
Revolutionary Armed Forces of Colombia	Kidnapping	Diplomatic Private citizens
Guerrilla Army of the Poor	Attacks on installations Kidnapping Bombing Shooting	Diplomatic Business Military Private citizens Government official Religious
Movement of April 19	Kidnapping	Diplomatic Private citizen
Japanese Red Army	Threats on installations	Diplomatic
PFLP	Bombings	Business
As-Sa'iqa	Assassinations	Diplomatic
Al Fatah	Barricade and hostage	Military
Black June	Hijackings Kidnapping	Private citizen
Red Brigades	Kidnapping	Military
Red Army Faction	Attacks on installations Bombings Shootings	Diplomatic Business Military Private citizen Transportation
Sendero Luminoso	Bombings	Diplomatic Business
Moro National Liberation Front	Kidnapping	Private citizen
Turkish groups(3)	Bombings Shooting	Diplomatic Military
Libyan agents	Assassination threats	Diplomatic
Islamic Jihad	Truck bombing Kidnapping Shooting	Military Private citizen Diplomatic Religious

Japanese Red Army, Palestinian groups, Libyan agents, and the Islamic Jihad.

None of these groups has carried out operations against American targets within the United States, and only the ASALA and the Libyans have conducted operations on U.S. soil. Palestinian groups have, however, been implicated in planned terrorist activity in the United States, Libyans were suspected of involvement in an assassination threat against U.S. officials in 1981, and the ASALA attacked Turkish, Swiss, and Canadian interests in the United States between 1980 and 1982.

The mobility of a terrorist group is an important indicator of capabilities and resources, because carrying out an operation abroad requires extensive planning and funds. Indicators of mobility (and potential mobility) include evidence of state support and direction, international links with other terrorist groups, and the type, frequency, and sophistication of past operations.

There is evidence that all five groups have state sponsorship, and all have demonstrated the ability to build and use contacts with other terrorist groups, sometimes obtaining logistical and personnel support. Capabilities demonstrated by past operations, however, probably constitute the most significant evidence of international potential.

The ASALA was at the peak of its activity in the early 1980s and has been relatively inactive since mid-1984. The group's willingness to engage in large-scale, indiscriminate operations was evinced in its July 1983 attack on the Turkish Airlines counter at Orly Airport in Paris, which killed 8 people and injured 55. The group split into two factions in July 1983, and the more radical faction has remained active. However, this group appears to lack resources as a result of the disruption of its headquarters in Lebanon, although it may receive some support from Syria and/or Iran. Strong ties with Palestinian groups may enable the ASALA to rebuild its base in Lebanon, but the lack of activity since 1984 indicates that the group has been seriously weakened. Moreover, its principal target is Turkey, and a shift in this focus is unlikely. Therefore, an ASALA assault on a U.S. nuclear facility is a distinctly remote possibility.

The Japanese Red Army has not conducted any terrorist operations since the 1970s. There were recent reports of activities by Japanese Red Army members in Lebanon, but no evidence of concerted group organization or activity. While the group is definitely linked to the Palestinians, state support appears to be indirect, i.e., channeled through the Palestinian factions. Having no demonstrable organizational capability or significant activity, much less a strong propensity to take action against the United States at home or abroad, the Japanese Red Army is also an unlikely nuclear adversary.

Palestinian groups are known to have received support from various countries in the Middle East, in the form of funds, training, intelligence, asylum, and moral support. A few Palestinian groups are considered responsible for most of the international links among terrorist groups today. These links are extensive and have been valuable assets in the past. Activity is now less frequent and less elaborate than in the past, however, for two main reasons: The groups are still recuperating from losses suffered during the 1982 Israeli invasion of Lebanon and there is considerable internal dissension; and some groups have shown a tendency to follow a political rather than a militaristic line.

Libyan agents have extensive support and direction from Libyan leader Muammar Qaddafi, as do other terrorist groups. Qaddafi's agents are thought to have been responsible for dozens of murders of Libyan dissidents in exile throughout the world. The resources, scope, and capabilities of these terrorists are formidable. Although there are no indications that Qaddafi has any interest in damaging or sabotaging a U.S. nuclear facility, there is considerable tension between the United States and Libya. Qaddafi has also repeatedly voiced interest in developing a Libyan nuclear capability. While this increases the likelihood of theft of nuclear-related information or material by Libyan agents, such assets could be more safely obtained through an insider than through an armed operation against a facility. There is nothing to indicate that Libyan agents are likely to attack a nuclear installation, but given that Qaddafi is an unstable factor in international affairs and that he has considerable resources, his involvement in an operation within the United States is something to consider.

Islamic Jihad is an elusive, amorphous enemy at this time. Syrian and Iranian state support and direction are generally assumed, and links with Lebanese groups are known to exist. Islamic Jihad has operational elements throughout the Middle East and apparently in Southern Europe, as well. Responsible for tremendous damage to the U.S. presence in Lebanon, the organization has demonstrated considerable technical skill as well as access to sophisticated equipment and materials. Its radical religious ideology puts it in complete opposition to the United States, and its determination, evidenced by suicidal truck bombers, makes it a dangerous adversary. Although the group has not strayed far out of the Middle East, its future actions depend largely upon American actions in the Middle East and Lebanon. While Islamic Jihad operations in the United States appear unlikely, such actions could occur in response to retaliatory action taken by the United States following a terrorist incident elsewhere in the world. A French retaliatory air strike against known terrorist camps in Lebanon in response to the bombing of French forces in Beirut resulted in further terrorist activity, this time on French soil.[1] Therefore, Islamic Jihad must be considered a candidate for the list of likely perpetrators of a nuclear assault.

Palestinian groups, particularly Black June, Al Fatah, and the Popular Front for the Liberation of Palestine (PFLP), have demonstrated willingness to attack American interests and the ability to carry out effective and deadly operations outside of the Middle East. They also have considerable state support. These groups are currently weakened and fragmented, which lessens the probability of elaborate international operations, but Palestinian terrorist activity is highly dependent on the course of U.S. involvement in the Arab-Israeli conflict. Thus, a Palestinian terrorist operation in this country cannot be confidently ruled out.

---

[1] The "Martyrs of Baalbek" claimed responsibility for bombings in Paris in January 1984.

V. CONCLUSION

The threat to U.S. nuclear programs has not changed significantly over the past decade. The main threats in the 1970s—malicious mischief, theft of special nuclear materials, sabotage, terrorism, and espionage—still exist today. However, increasing state sponsorship of terrorism and the changing nature and increased visibility of protests against nuclear weapons both in the United States and abroad could have a significant impact on the security of U.S. nuclear weapons and facilities.

The total volume of worldwide activity has grown since 1980, and terrorist incidents have become increasingly lethal. State sponsorship puts more resources (money, sophisticated munitions, enhanced intelligence, logistical support, and technical expertise) into the hands of the terrorists. State support, therefore, may have potentially serious consequences for the security of U.S. nuclear facilities and programs, especially in light of possible nuclear weapons proliferation. Sophisticated, well-armed, well-financed, and well-led terrorist organizations comparable to elite commando units are now a reality, and this type of organization could be employed by a state sponsor to steal nuclear materials. In addition, terrorists may offer themselves as mercenaries for such tasks. Whereas the visibly heavy defenses of such installations may have dissuaded terrorists in the past, the greater resources afforded by state sponsors could make such operations feasible and attractive to terrorist groups.

However, despite the growing volume of international terrorism, there is still relatively little terrorist activity within the United States. According to FBI statistics, there were only 29 terrorist incidents recorded in the United States in 1980, 42 in 1981, 51 in 1982, 31 in 1983, and 13 in 1984. (These statistics do not include abortion-clinic bombings, 21 of which occurred during 1984.) Specific issue-oriented terrorism could have an effect on this country's nuclear programs, but trends in such activity suggest that visible physical security measures at nuclear facilities remain a significant deterrent.

In the United States, unlike other countries, the major threat emanates from individuals who are motivated by personal reasons (financial gain, revenge, etc.) or who have or desire access to inside information. Hostile nuclear-facility employees obviously fall into this category.

The paucity of recent anti-nuclear activity in the United States and the failure of foreign agitations and terrorist activities to manifest themselves here should not obscure the potential threat these trends could represent. Increased visibility of American nuclear programs could make them inviting targets for disruptive and destructive missions. The increased resources of state-sponsored terrorists (and the concomitant use by states of terrorists as instruments of national policy) should alert policymakers against any relaxation of the safeguards regimen. Renewed analysis of nuclear safeguards should be actively considered, even though current trends do not indicate any immediate or pressing danger.

BIBLIOGRAPHY

Bass, Gail, et al., *The Appeal of Nuclear Crimes to the Spectrum of Potential Adversaries,* The Rand Corporation, R-2803-SL, February 1982.

——, *Motivations and Possible Actions of Potential Criminal Adversaries of U.S. Nuclear Programs,* The Rand Corporation, R-2554-SL, February 1980.

Bontwell, Jeffrey, "Politics and the Peace Movement in Western Germany," *International Security,* Vol. 7, No. 4, Spring 1983.

Brinkley, Joel, "Methods and Aims Point to a New Breed of Spy," *The New York Times,* June 9, 1985.

Burnham, David, "The Case of the Missing Uranium," *The Atlantic Monthly,,* Vol. 243, No. 4, April 1979.

——, "House Aide Tells of Suspicion U.S. Uranium Was Stolen Ten Years Ago," *The New York Times,* August 9, 1977.

——, "1968 Mystery of a Vanished Ship: Did Its Uranium End Up in Israel?" *The New York Times,* April 29, 1977.

——, "U.S. Agencies Suspected Missing Uranium Went to Israel for Arms," *The New York Times,* November 6, 1977.

Butterfield, Fox, "Anatomy of the Nuclear Protest," *The New York Times Magazine,* July 11, 1984.

Cordes, Bonnie, et al., *Trends in International Terrorism, 1982 and 1983,* The Rand Corporation, R-3183-SL, August 1984.

deLeon, Peter, "Freeze: The Literature of the Nuclear Weapons Debate," *Journal of Conflict Resolution,* Vol. 27, No. 1, March 1983.

deLeon, Peter, et al., *Attributes of Potential Criminal Adversaries of U.S. Nuclear Programs,* The Rand Corporation, R-2225-SL, February 1978.

Erskine, Hazel Gandet, "The Polls: Atomic Weapons and Nuclear Energy," *Public Opinion Quarterly,* Vol. 27, No. 2, Summer 1963.

"The Freeze Issue Has Reagan on the Spot," *Business Week,* May 16, 1983.

Gillette, Robert, "200 Tons of Uranium Lost; Israel May Have It," *Los Angeles Times,* April 29, 1977.

Goshko, John M., "Israel Got U.S.-Made Devices," *Washington Post,* April 14, 1985.

——, "L.A. Man Indicted in Export of Potential Nuclear Bomb Component to Israel," *Washington Post,* May 17, 1985.

Hersh, Seymour M., "A Pakistani Tried to Send Trigger for A-Bomb Home," *The New York Times*, February 25, 1985.

Hiatt, Fred, "Edging Toward Nuclear Doom: Several Nations Reported Moving Toward the Bomb," *Washington Post*, October 31, 1984.

"Hindu-Jew 'Conspiracy' Prepares Attack on Atomic Installation," *Nawa-I-Waqt*, LaHore, September 16, 1984 (JPRS-NEA-84-160, October 26, 1984).

Hoffman, Bruce, *Commando Raids: 1946–1983*, The Rand Corporation, N-2316-USDP, October 1985.

Jenkins, Brian M., *Embassies Under Siege: A Review of 48 Embassy Takeovers, 1971–1980*, The Rand Corporation, R-2651-RC, January 1981.

———, *Will Terrorists Go Nuclear?* The Rand Corporation, P-5541, November 1975.

———, *Terrorism and the Nuclear Safeguards Issue*, The Rand Corporation, P-5611, March 1976.

Kirkwood, Craig W., and Stephen M. Pollack, *Methodology for Characterizing Potential Adversaries of Nuclear Safeguards Systems*, San Francisco: Woodward-Clyde for Lawrence Livermore Laboratories, 1978.

Kraemer, Bernard M., et al., "Attitudes Towards Nuclear Weapons and Nuclear War: 1945–1982," *Journal of Social Issues*, Vol. 39, No. 1, 1983.

Nelkin, Dorothy, and Michael Pollack, *The Atom Besieged*, Cambridge, Massachusetts: The MIT Press, 1982.

Oberdorfer, Don, "Pakistan Concerned About Attack on Atomic Plants," *Washington Post*, October 12, 1984.

Perlmutter, Amos, "The Israeli Raid on Iraq: A New Proliferation Landscape," *Strategic Review*, Vol. 10, No. 1, Winter 1982.

Pilgrim, Michael K., and R. William Mengel, *Handbook for Development of Deterrent Strategies*, BMD for U.S. Department of Energy, September 1981.

Ramberg, Bennett, *An Unrecognized Military Peril*, Berkeley: University of California Press, 1984.

Reinstedt, R. N., and Judith Westbury, *Major Crimes as Analogs to Potential Threats to Nuclear Facilities and Programs*, The Rand Corporation, N-1498-SL, April 1980.

Russett, Bruce M., "Ethical Dilemmas of Nuclear Deterrence," *International Security*, Vol. 8, No. 4, Spring 1984.

Scarborough, J. C., and C. A. Russell, *Nuclear Plant Security in the 1980s-90s*, paper delivered at the American Nuclear Society, Atlanta, Georgia, June 1979.

Steward, John B., Jr., et al., *Generic Adversary Characteristics: Summary Report,* U.S. Nuclear Regulatory Commission, NUREG-0459, March 1979.

Tempest, Rone, "Gandhi Says FBI Should Have Told Him Sooner of Terrorist Death Plot," *Los Angeles Times,* June 5, 1985.

Tyler, Tom R., and Kathleen M. McGraw, "The Threat of Nuclear War: Risk Interpretations and Behavioral Responses," *Journal of Social Issues,* Vol. 39, No. 1, 1983.

United States Congress, Office of Technology Assessment, *Nuclear Proliferation and Safeguards,* U.S. Government Printing Office, Washington, D.C., 1976; also New York: Praeger, 1977.

van Voorst, L. Bruce. "The Critical Masses," *Foreign Policy,* No. 48, Fall 1982.

Wagner, N. E., *A Survey of Threat Studies Relating to the Nuclear Power Industry,* Sandia Laboratories, August 1977.

Working Party under the Chairmanship of the Bishop of Salisbury, *The Church and the Bomb: Nuclear Weapons and Christian Conscience,* London: Hodder & Stoughton, 1982.

Worner, Manfred, "The 'Peace Movement' and NATO: An Alternative View from Bonn," *Strategic Review,* Vol. 10, No. 1, Winter 1982.

Yankelovich, Daniel, and John Doble, "Nuclear Weapons and the U.S.S.R.: The Public Mood," *Foreign Affairs,* Vol. 3, No. 1, Fall 1984.

Steinbruner, John D., "Nuclear Decisionmaking: Choices About Weapons," in Burns, Richard Dean, ed., *Encyclopedia of Arms Control and Disarmament*, Vol. II. New York: Charles Scribner's Sons, 1993.

Taubman, Philip. "Gas Drifting From Ship, but Have-Told Him Leaves in Tornado Path," *New York Times*, July 5, 1985.

Tyler, Tom R., and Kathleen M. McGraw, "The Threat of Nuclear War: Risk Interpretation and Behavioral Response," *Journal of Social Issues*, Vol. 39, No. 1, 1983.

United States Congress, Office of Technology Assessment, *Nuclear Proliferation and Safeguards*. U.S. Government Printing Office, Washington D.C., 1977; also New York: Praeger, 1977.

Van Voorst, L. Bruce. "The United Nations: Force for Peace," No. 40, Fall 1982.

Weymouth, Lally. "Nuclear Threat: Steps in Reacting to the Nuclear Emergency," *Media Manufacturers*, August 1987.

Wogaman, Phil, ed. *The Relationship of the Bishop of Salisbury: The Challenge and the Bishop's Letter, Reagan's and Christian Conscience*. Lanham: Rowman & Littlefield, 1984.

Wolpert, Ms. "The Peace Movement and NATO: An Alternative View," *Political European Affairs*, Vol. 10, No. 1, Winter 1982.

Zur, Ofer, Edward, and Terry P. K. "Nuclear Weapons and the U.S.S.R.: The Unthinkable?" *The Humanities*, Vol. 3, No. 1, Fall 1985.